P9-CQR-623

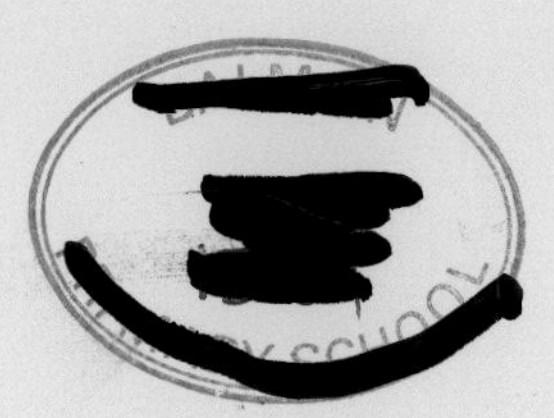

Nuclear Energy

Editor: John Clark
Editorial Planning Clark Robinson Ltd
Design: David West
Children's Book Design
Illustrator: Peter Bull
Picture research: Cecilia Weston-Baker
Photographic Credits:
Cover and pages 8 and 19 both: UKAEA; pages 4-5, 9, 11 both, 12, 20, 21 and 25: British Nuclear Fuels Ltd; page 13; Dounreay Power Station; pages 23 left and 30 top: Science Photo Library; page 23 bottom: Rex Features; page 29: Topham Picture Library: page 30 bottom: British Gas.

Created and designed by
Aladdin Books Ltd
28 Percy Street
London W1P 9FF

First published in
Great Britain in 1990 by
Gloucester Press
96 Leonard Street
London EC2A 4RH

ISBN 0-7496-0369-0

Printed in Belgium

The publishers would like to acknowledge that the photographs reproduced within this book have been posed by models or have been obtained from photographic agencies.

A CIP catalogue record for this book is available from the British Library

Facts on

Nuclear Energy

Guy Arnold

GLOUCESTER PRESS
London · New York · Toronto · Sydney

CONTENTS

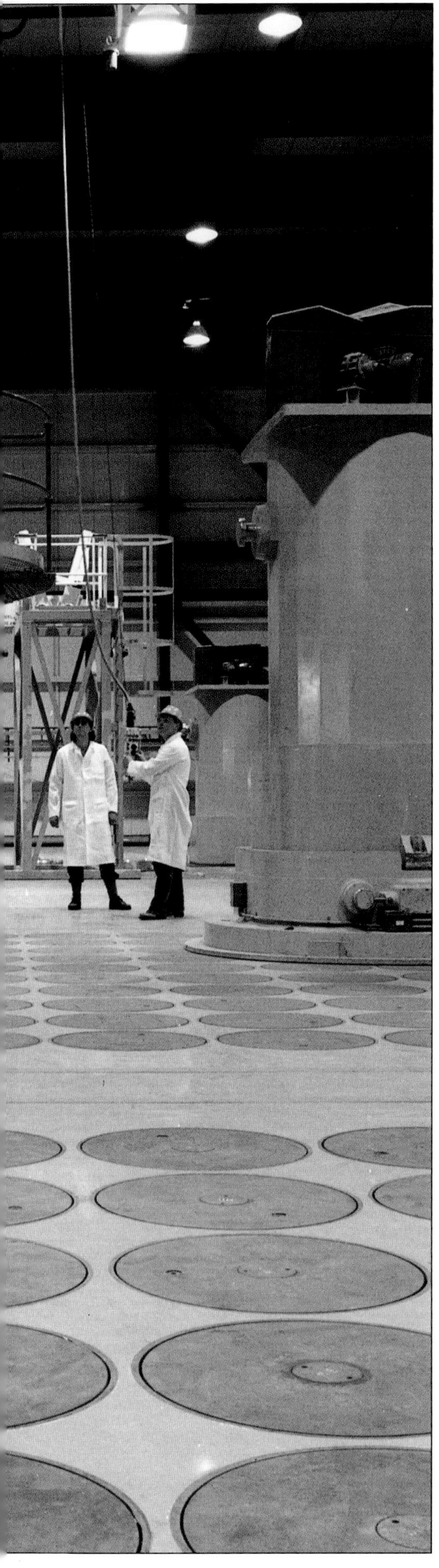

INTRODUCTION

Nuclear power is now an important source of energy for many countries in the world. But until quite recently, most people had never heard of nuclear energy. People first became aware of it when two atomic bombs were dropped on Hiroshima and Nagasaki in Japan at the end of World War II. Since that time, nuclear energy has only been used to create power supplies – although there are many nuclear weapons in the world.

The world's population is increasing rapidly, and people are demanding higher standards of living. Both of these lead to an increasing need for energy. This energy is needed for many things, such as driving machinery in factories, light and heating. At the same time as the world's energy needs are increasing, supplies of fossil fuels (coal, oil and gas) are running out. These are the world's main sources of power. Alternative sources have to be found. One alternative that has already been found is nuclear power.

◁ Nuclear plant at Windscale UK

6 POWER OF THE ATOM

Nuclear energy is sometimes also called atomic energy. Nuclear energy is created when the dense core of an atom (called the nucleus) is split. This process is known as nuclear fission. The nucleus of an atom is made up of two types of particles called protons and neutrons. These particles are bound together very strongly. It is very difficult to break up nuclei, although the larger ones are easier to split. If a nucleus is broken up, three things happen: the nuclei of different elements with smaller nuclei are made; atomic particles are released; and energy is produced. There is also a process called nuclear fusion in which nuclei are joined together. This also gives off energy, but is not used in power stations as scientists have yet to find a way of controlling it effectively.

Uncontrolled nuclear reaction

CONTROLLED AND UNCONTROLLED

In nuclear fission, a nucleus is split when it captures a free-moving neutron that has come from radioactive material. A nucleus that is split by one neutron produces more neutrons. These are then captured by more nuclei, which produce yet more neutrons, and so on. This is known as a chain reaction.

In a controlled nuclear reaction, most of the new neutrons do not hit another nucleus. As a result, the chain reaction does not spread to many other nuclei, and only a limited amount of energy is produced. This is what happens in the reactors of nuclear power stations.

In an uncontrolled reaction most of the new neutrons hit other nuclei, many atoms are split and an enormous amount of energy is released. This is what happens in atomic bombs.

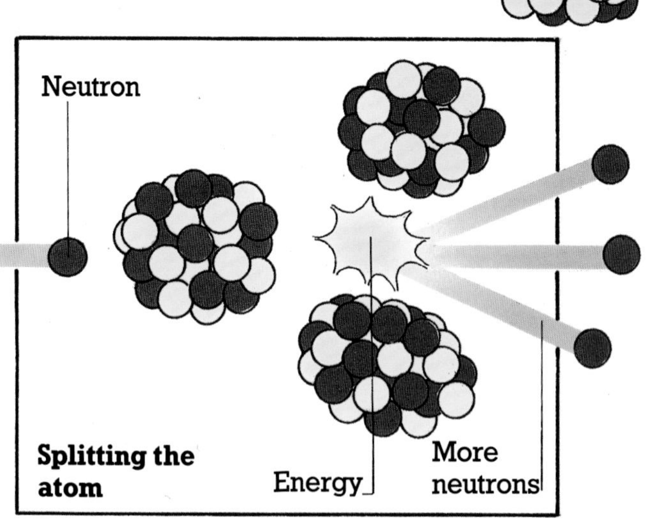

Splitting the atom

Controlled nuclear reaction

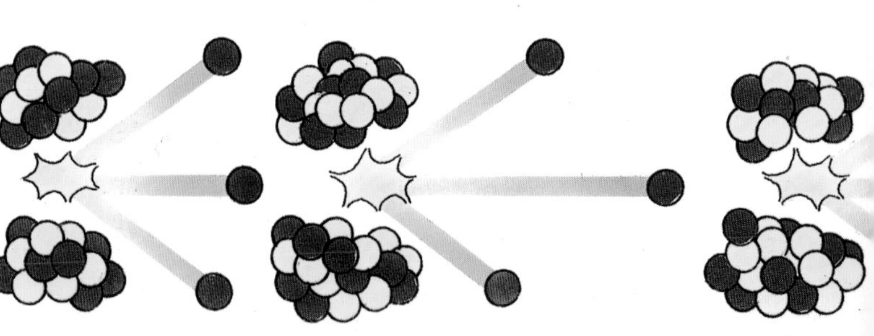

THE BOMB

An atom bomb (fission bomb) is an uncontrolled nuclear reaction. Because neutrons move so fast and the nuclei split so quickly, the vast amount of energy is all released in less than a second. The only two atomic bombs used in warfare were dropped on Japan at the end of World War II.

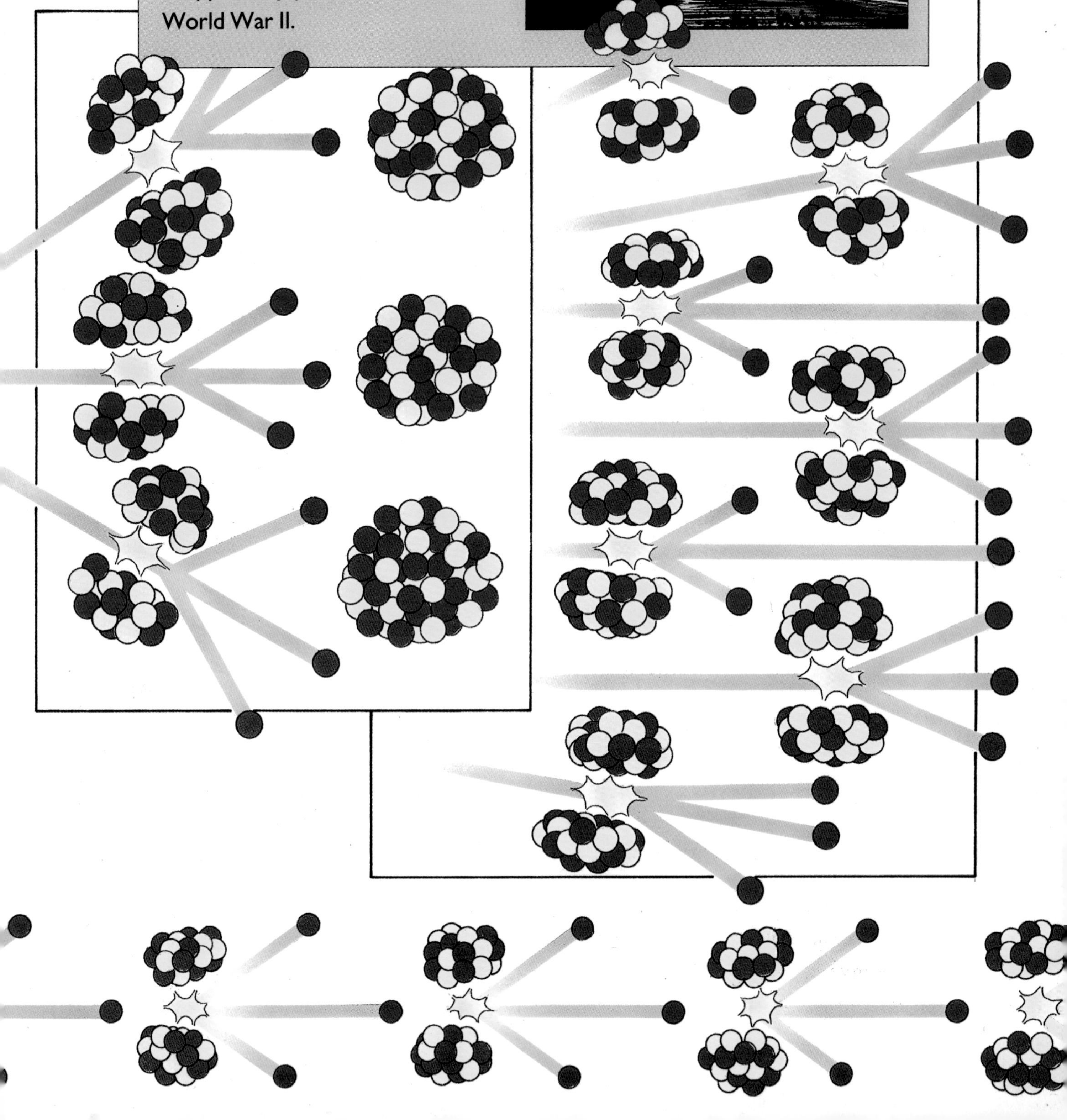

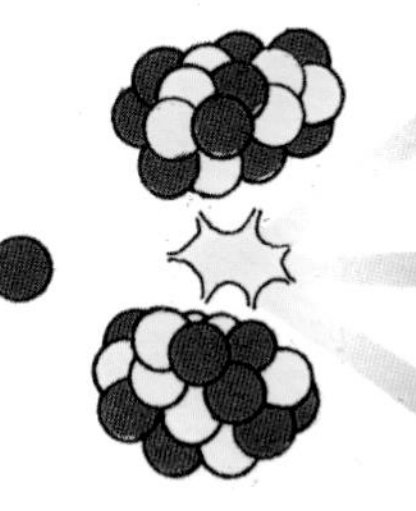

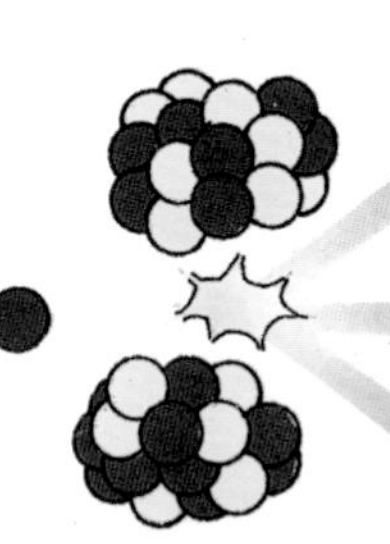

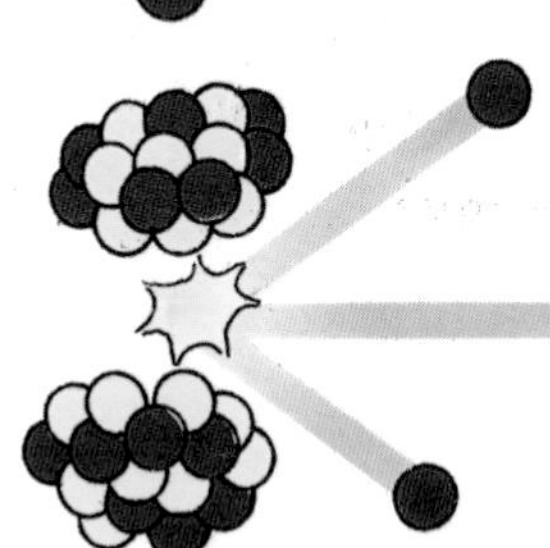

8 NUCLEAR FUELS

Only atoms of certain elements have nuclei that give off neutrons when they are split, and so only these elements can be used to create a nuclear reaction. They are known as fissile materials. The only naturally occurring fissile material is a particular form of uranium, the isotope called uranium-235 (or U-235). Isotopes are forms of elements with different numbers of neutrons in their nuclei. Uranium is a dense shiny metal with the heaviest atomic weight of any naturally occurring element. Only a very small part of the uranium that is found – seven parts in a thousand – is U-235. The rest is the isotope U-238. One kilogram of U-235 gives as much energy as 3 million kilograms of coal. Other nuclear fuels can be made by the conversion and processing of uranium.

MINING

Two parts in a million of the Earth's crust is uranium. Uranium is found as ores, which are minerals that can be mined. In most areas, concentrations of uranium in the earth are very low, so that it is only worth mining in a few places. The main areas where it is mined are in Zaire, South Africa, France, Czechoslovakia, North America, Australia, China and the Soviet Union.

Uranium ore is found both near the surface and deep underground. It is mined in the same way as other ores.

SEPARATION AND RODS

Before uranium can be used, the U-235 has to be separated from the U-238. The uranium is converted into a gas, which is then put into a centrifuge – a cylinder that spins very fast.

The heavier U-238 goes to the edge and the lighter U-235 stays at the centre.

The U-235 is then converted into a black powder called uranium dioxide. This is made into small pellets, packed into tubes called pins. The pins are bundled into larger tubes and are ready to put into the reactor.

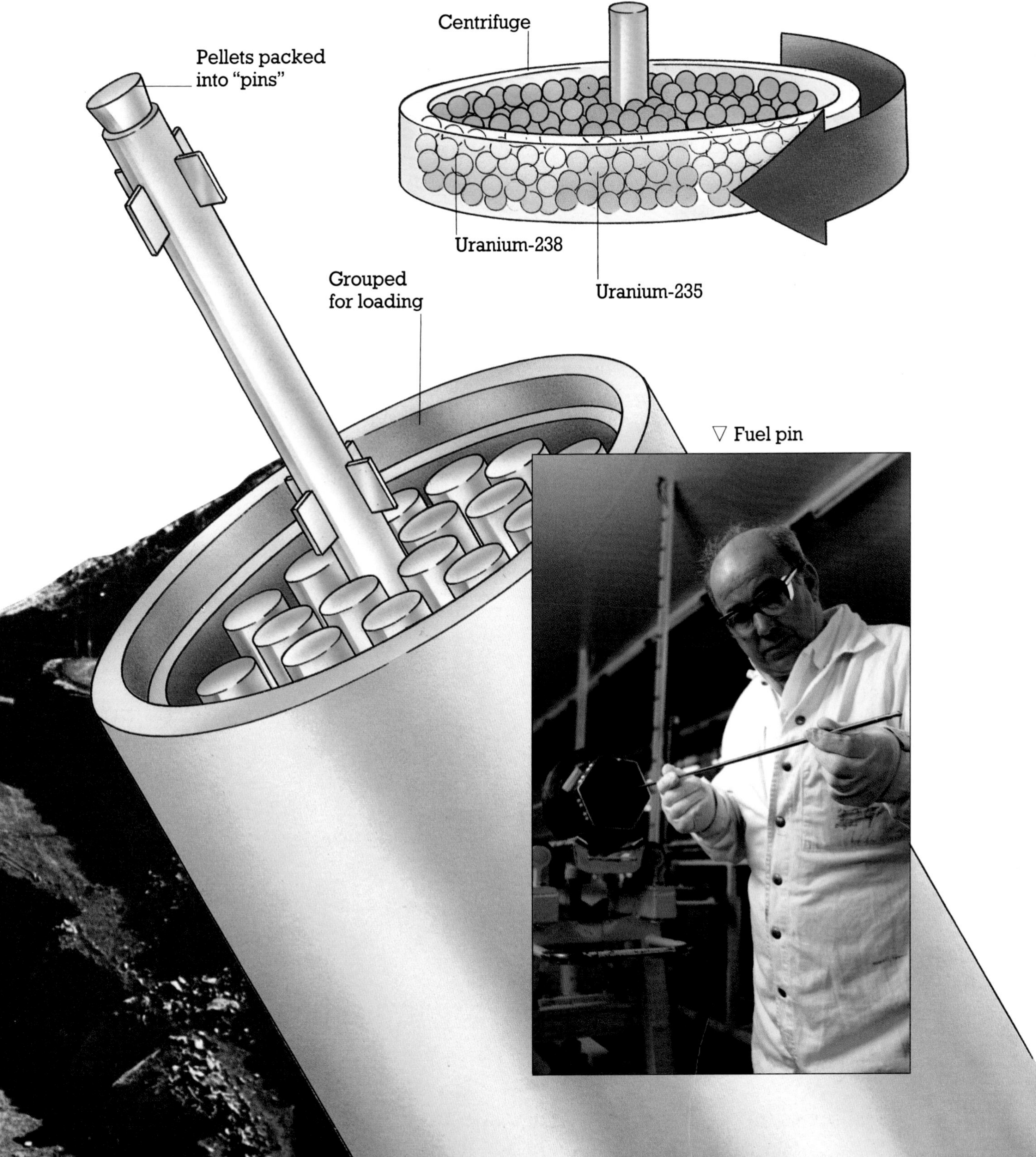

▽ Fuel pin

POWER STATION

In a conventional thermal power station, coal or oil is burned to turn water into steam which then drives turbines for generating electricity. But in a nuclear power station, the heat for making steam comes from a controlled nuclear reaction. The reaction takes place in the pressure vessel inside the containment building. The containment building is one of the main differences between a conventional and a nuclear power station. It is made of thick concrete and steel and is necessary to help prevent the risk of any radioactivity escaping – either in the normal running of the station or if there was an accident. Another difference is that some nuclear power stations can be used to make the plutonium needed for nuclear bombs – especially some of the older stations.

THE SET-UP

A nuclear power station contains a nuclear reactor. In the reactor's core, fuel rods hold uranium, and control rods are moved in or out to control the number of neutrons that bring about fission in the fuel rods. The control rods absorb neutrons and if necessary can stop the chain reaction altogether. The nuclear reaction produces heat, and a coolant flows through the reactor, absorbs the heat and carries it off to a heat exchanger (or steam generator), where it is used to make steam. The power station then works like a conventional one: the steam drives a turbine, and the turbine drives a generator that produces electricity. Waste steam goes to the cooling towers to be condensed back into water.

Power out
Electricity is carried away from the power station by overhead power lines.

REACTOR FLOOR

The control or working area above the reactor (in the photograph below) gives access to the fuel rods and reactor core. Machines (below) can replace spent fuel rods with new ones without shutting down the reactor and stopping electricity production.

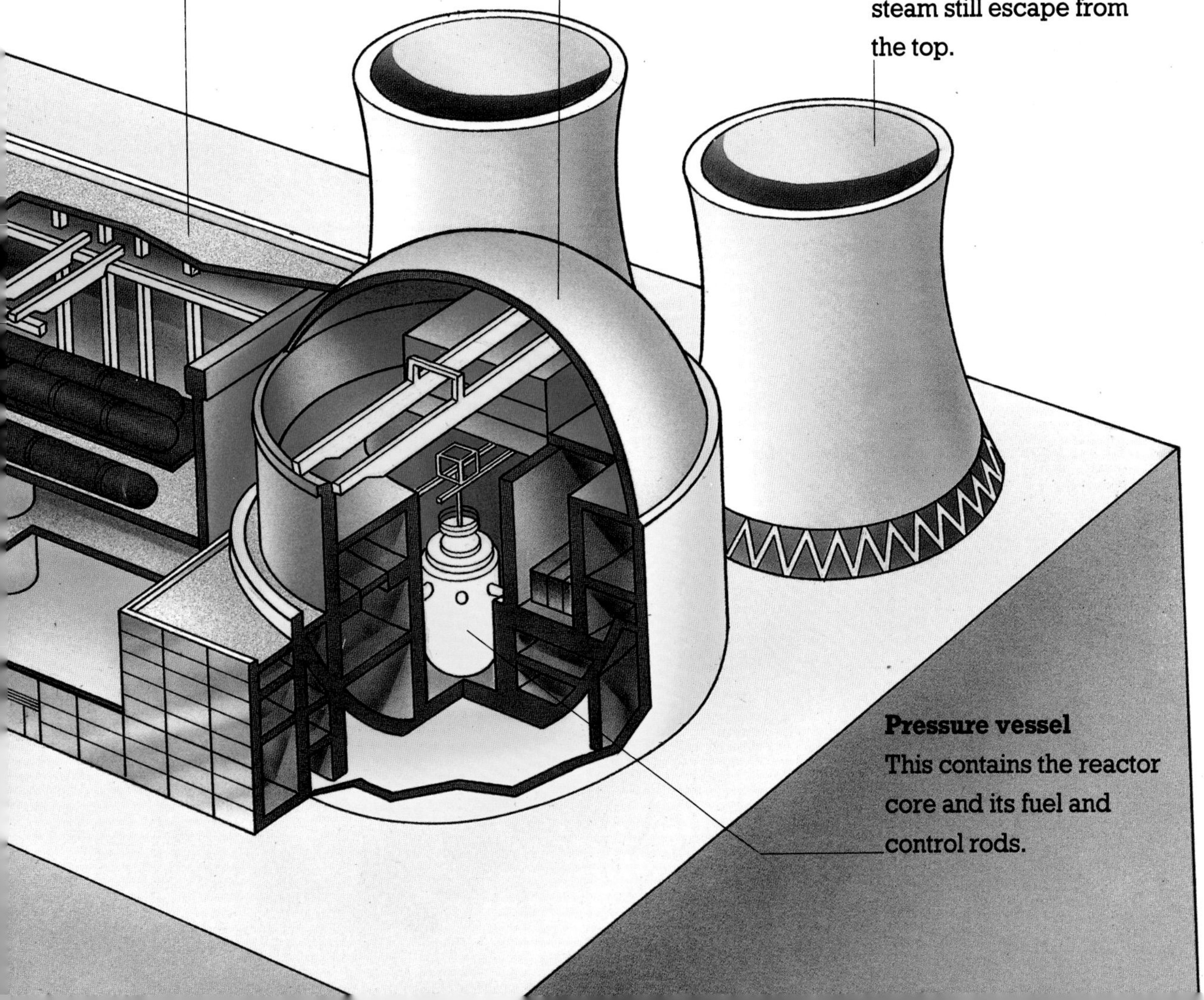

Turbine hall
Turbines are driven by high-pressure steam to make electricity.

Containment building
The reactor is surrounded by thick reinforced concrete.

Cooling towers
Waste steam is condensed back into water. But clouds of steam still escape from the top.

Pressure vessel
This contains the reactor core and its fuel and control rods.

NUCLEAR POWER STATION

CONTROL ROOM

The control room is the nerve centre of a nuclear reactor. Panels of instruments indicate every part of the operation. If there is any sign of danger – overheating of the core, for example – the reactor can be shut down in only a few seconds.

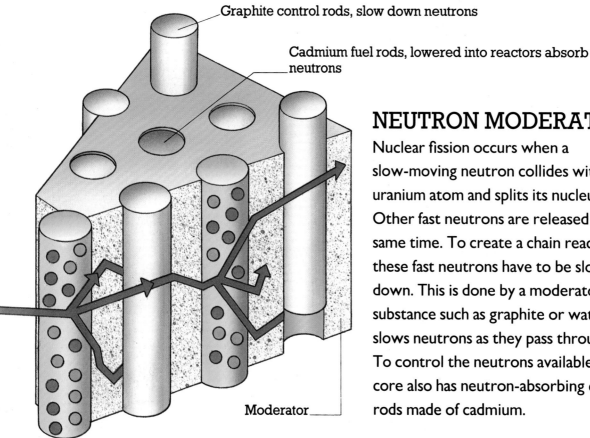

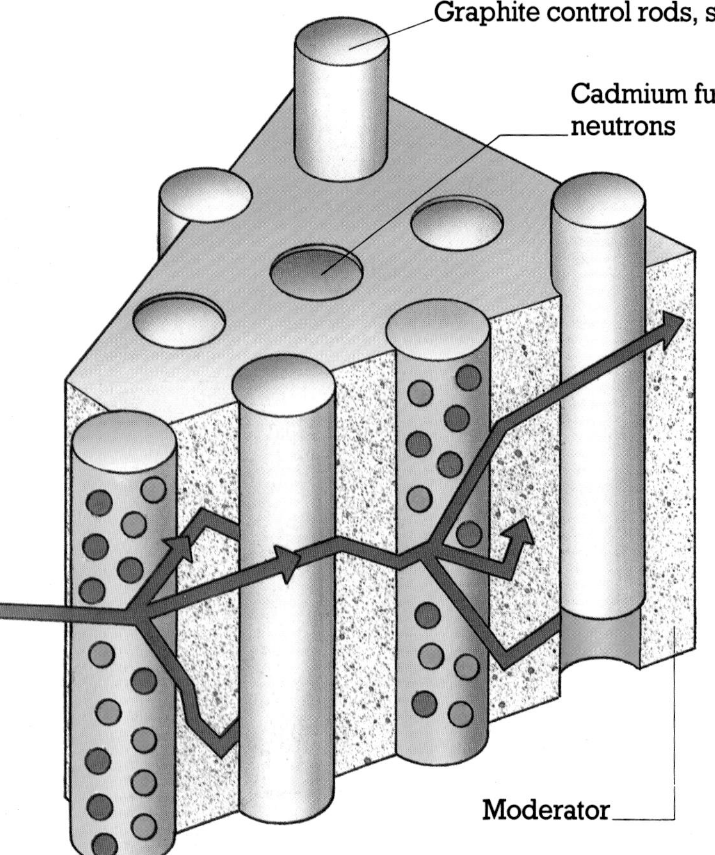

NEUTRON MODERATORS

Nuclear fission occurs when a slow-moving neutron collides with a uranium atom and splits its nucleus. Other fast neutrons are released at the same time. To create a chain reaction, these fast neutrons have to be slowed down. This is done by a moderator – a substance such as graphite or water that slows neutrons as they pass through it. To control the neutrons available, the core also has neutron-absorbing control rods made of cadmium.

FAST BREEDER

A breeder reactor has no moderator, but the fuel rods are packed more tightly. This results in very high temperatures that are controlled by using a liquid metal coolant. The fuel consists of uranium-238 with a little plutonium-239. The nuclear reaction converts the uranium into more plutonium, and in this way the reactor "breeds" plutonium.

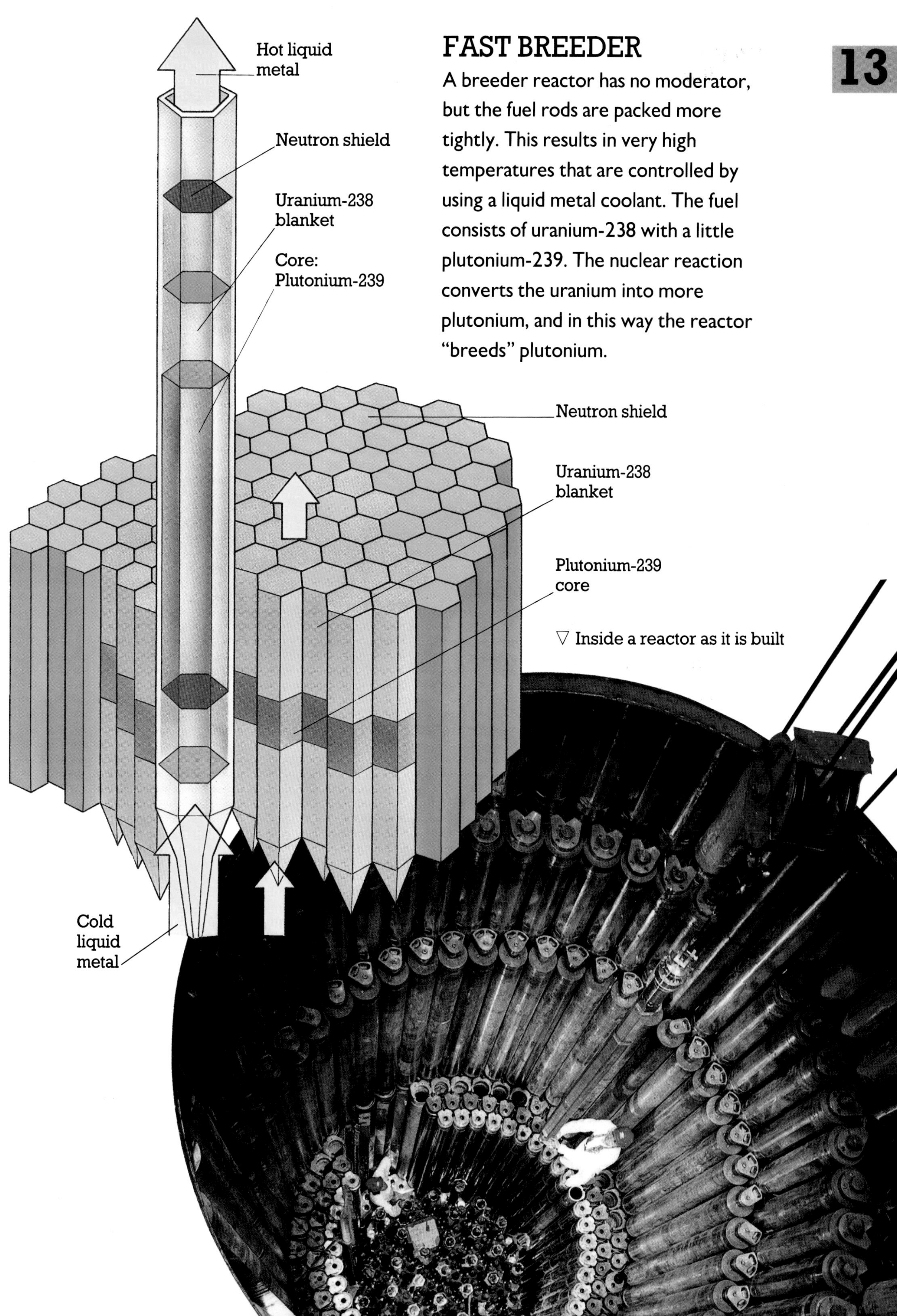

▽ Inside a reactor as it is built

TYPES OF STATION

Many different kinds of reactor have been developed as scientists have looked for the most efficient and safest way of controlling nuclear reactions. There are two main ways that nuclear reactors can differ: how the reaction is moderated or controlled and the type of reaction that takes place in the reactor vessel (or pressure vessel); and the way in which the reactor is cooled and the heat extracted to make steam. The main types of reaction are described in the previous pages. The different ways of cooling reactors are described below. Some reactors have been designed only for experiments and a few have a purely military purpose – to produce plutonium for atom bombs – but the great majority of nuclear reactors are built for commercial use to produce electricity.

BOILING WATER

The boiling water reactor (BWR) is cooled by water, which is turned into steam in the reactor. Unlike other sorts of reactor, the steam can go straight to the turbines that make electricity.

PRESSURIZED WATER

In a pressurized water reactor (PWR) water circulates under high pressure. The hot pressurized water turns ordinary water into steam in the steam generator.

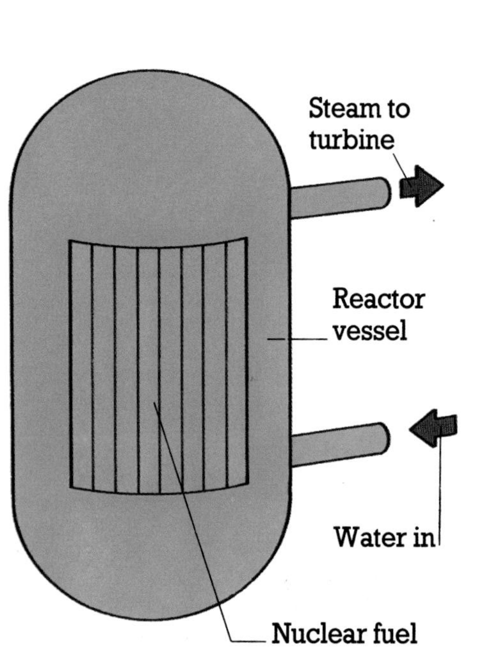

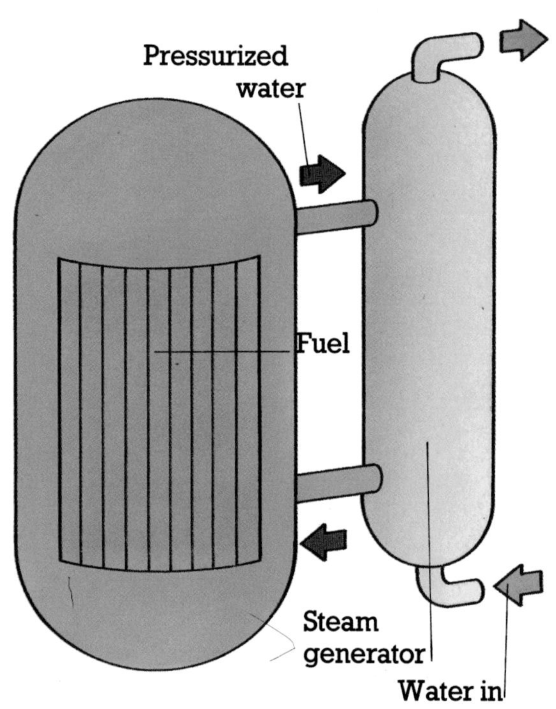

GENERATING

A generator in a power station works on the same principle as that in the arrangement below, although on a much larger scale! The drive wheel rotates a coil in a magnetic field. This makes an electric current in the coil. The current passes into the circuit by way of "brushes" that connect to the wires from the coil.

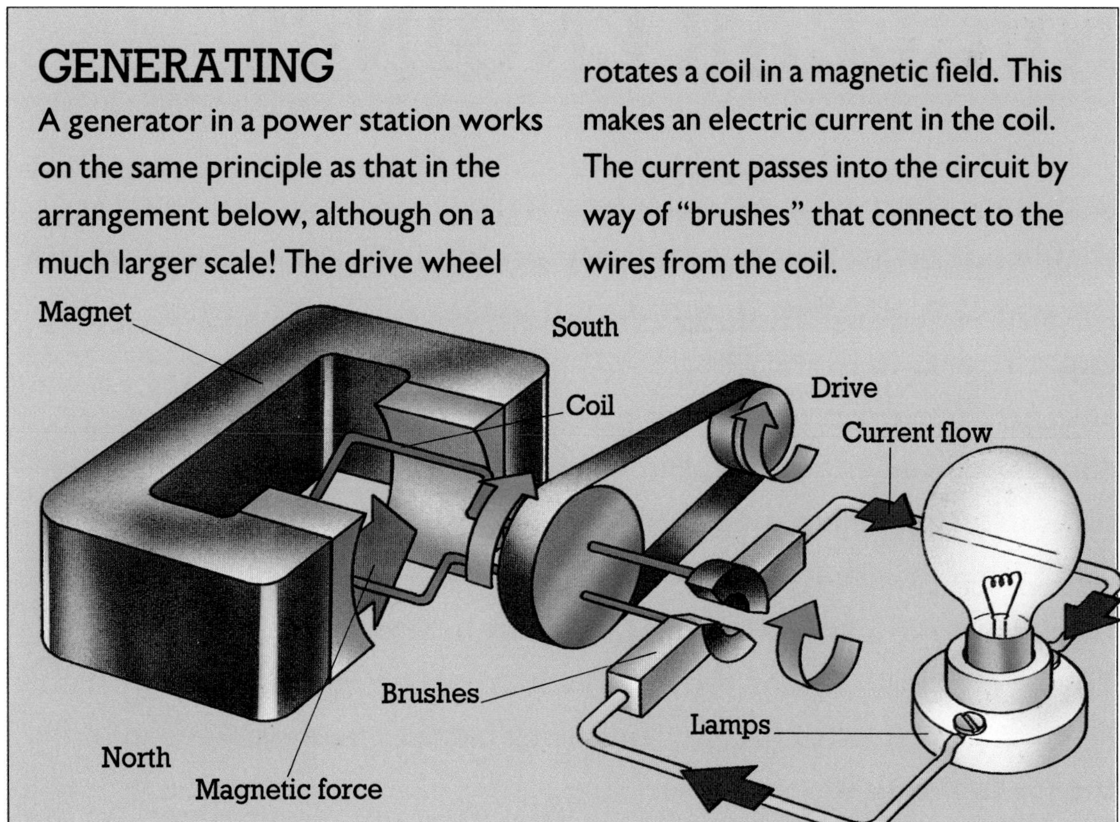

GAS-COOLED

A gas-cooled reactor uses gas – such as carbon dioxide or helium – as the coolant. Hot gas from the reactor vessel goes to a steam generator similar to the one in a pressurized water reactor.

LIQUID-METAL

Some breeder reactors use liquid metal (sodium) as the coolant. The hot sodium goes to a heat exchanger where it heats more sodium. This then goes to a steam generator.

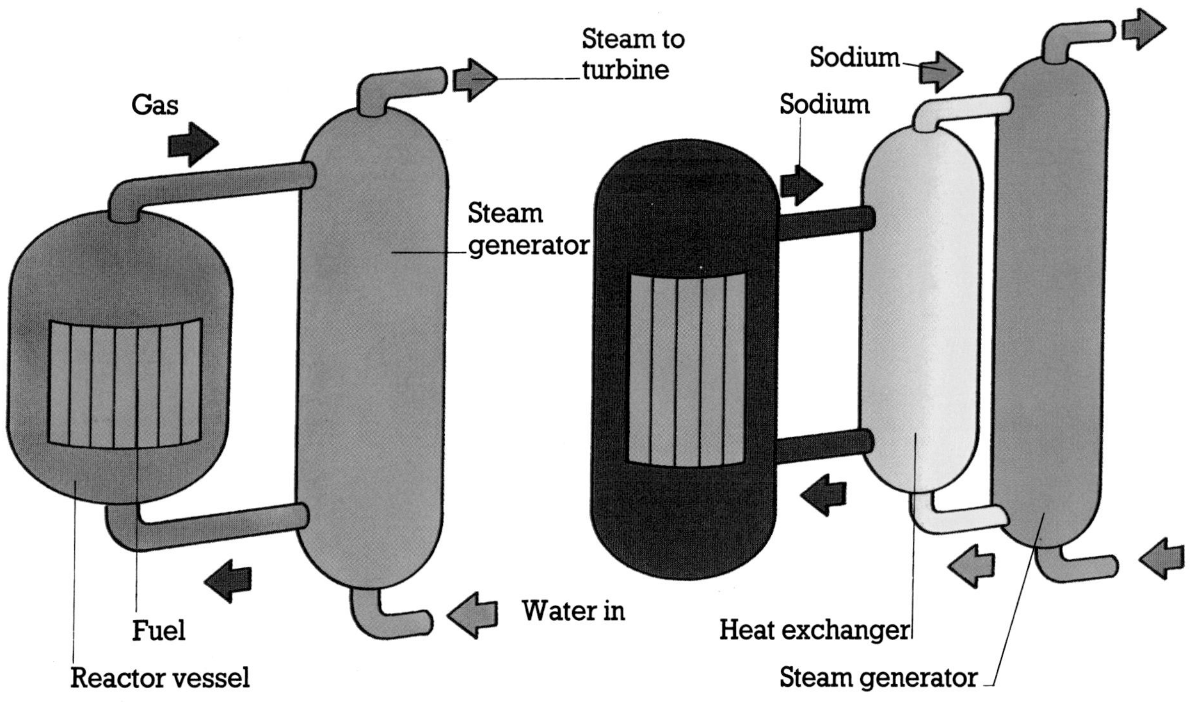

NUCLEAR ENGINES

In theory, there is no reason why different-sized nuclear reactors should not be used to drive almost any kind of engine. Shortly after the end of World War II, the United States Air Force began experiments to make a reactor that could be used to propel aircraft. The experiment was given up because it was becoming too dangerous and expensive. But nuclear reactors are now used very successfully to drive submarines and ships. The great advantage of using a nuclear reactor to provide the power is that the vessel can stay at sea for a very long time without having to dock to refuel. The photograph below shows a nuclear-powered ice-breaker. Ice-breakers use a lot of fuel because they have to push so hard against the ice to break it.

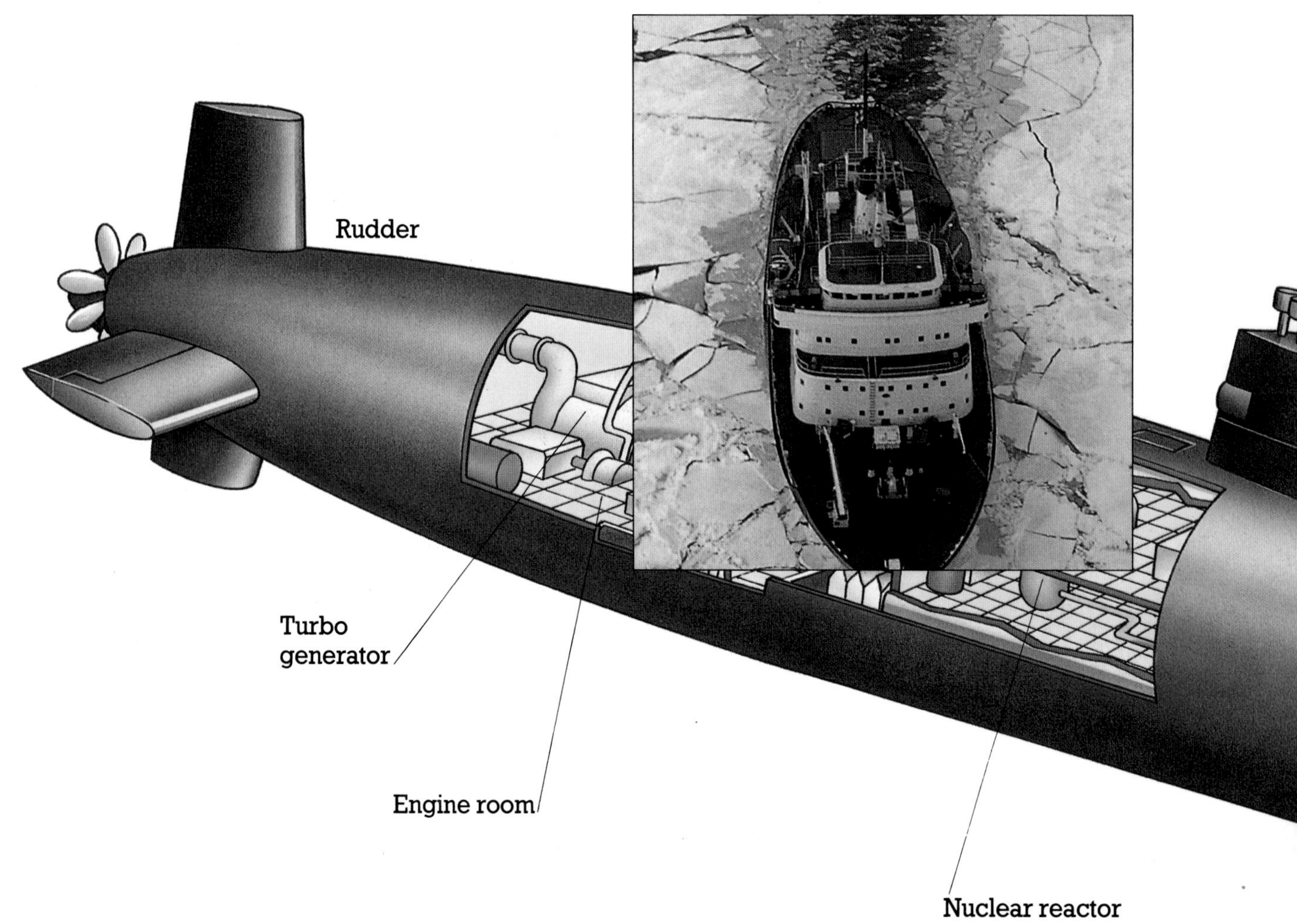

NUCLEAR SPACE PROBES

Nuclear power would be very useful for space probes that are sent far away from Earth. This is because it is impossible to refuel them. Long distance space flights need large amounts of energy. Small nuclear reactors have been studied to see whether they could provide this energy. Experiments have also been done to make a nuclear engine that could propel rockets.

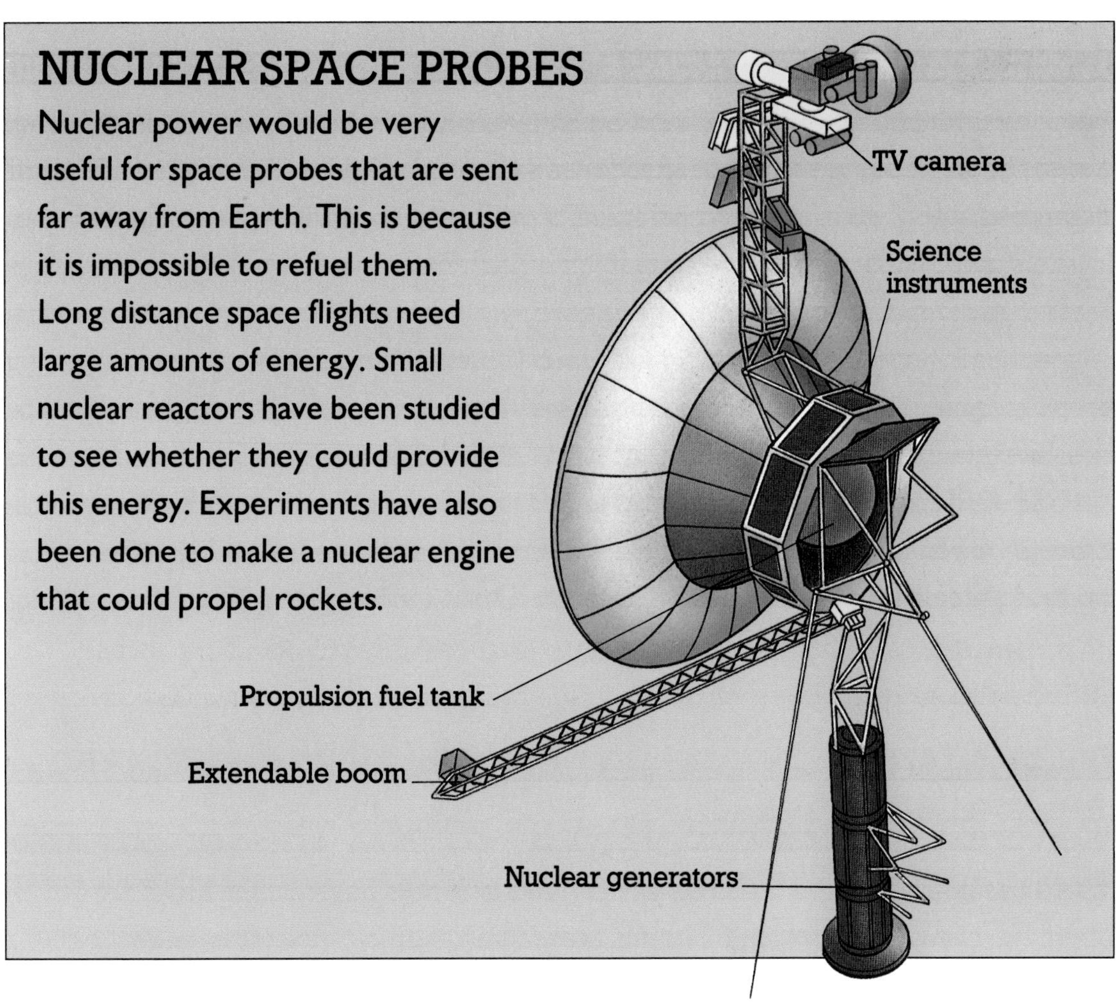

NUCLEAR SUBMARINES

People in the United States in 1946 started to study the idea of using nuclear reactors to power submarines. The studies were very successful. They led to the voyage of the nuclear submarine, *Nautilus*, to the North Pole underneath the ice in 1958. There are many advantages to nuclear submarines. The main advantage is that they can stay under water for a very long time. This is important if you do not want anyone to know that the submarine is there!

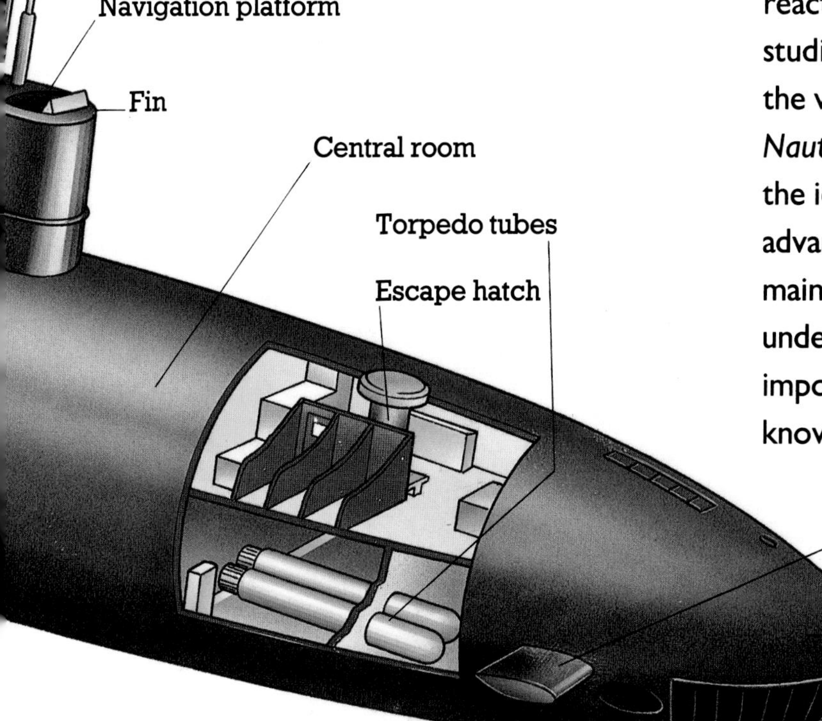

RADIATION

Radiation is produced when the nucleus of an atom decays or is split into two or more parts. Certain atoms, such as those of radium, decay naturally to produce radiation. This is known as radioactive decay. Nuclear fission, in which nuclei are split in a reactor, produces radioactive decay artificially.

There are three main sorts of radiation: alpha particles, beta particles and gamma rays. Alpha particles are relatively large and do not pass through material easily. They can be stopped by a sheet of paper. Beta particles are smaller and can be stopped by a thin sheet of metal, such as aluminium. Gamma-rays are like very high-energy X-rays. They can only be stopped by a thick sheet of a very dense metal, such as lead.

RADIOACTIVE ISOTOPES

Some atoms exist in more than one form. The difference is the number of neutrons in the nucleus. The forms of an element are known as its isotopes. Some isotopes are radioactive and others are not. Isotopes are given names such as uranium-235 (235 is the number of neutrons in the nucleus). Nuclear fission produces several radioactive isotopes.

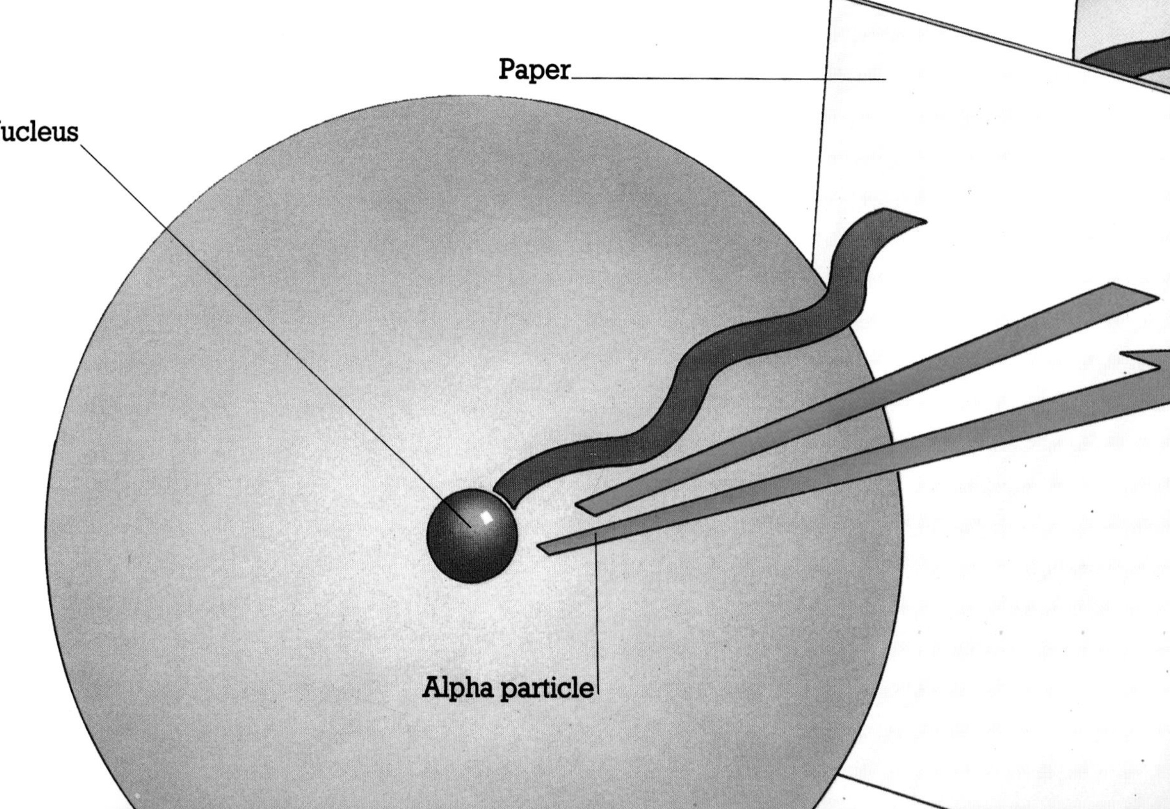

HANDLING

Radiation can cause a lot of harm to living things. Because of this, people who work in nuclear power stations have to be very careful to avoid radiation. Many radioactive materials have to be handled using remote control machines.

CHECKING RADIATION

It is not possible to see, smell or touch radiation. Special devices are needed to detect it. One such device is a Geiger counter. It can be used to check whether materials are radioactive.

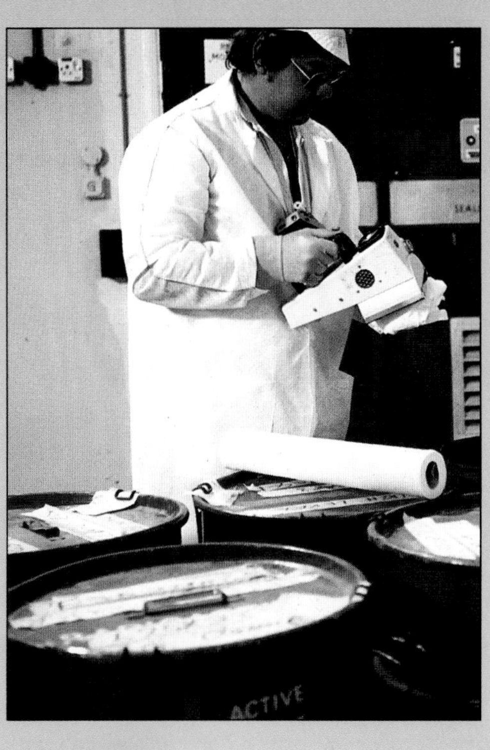

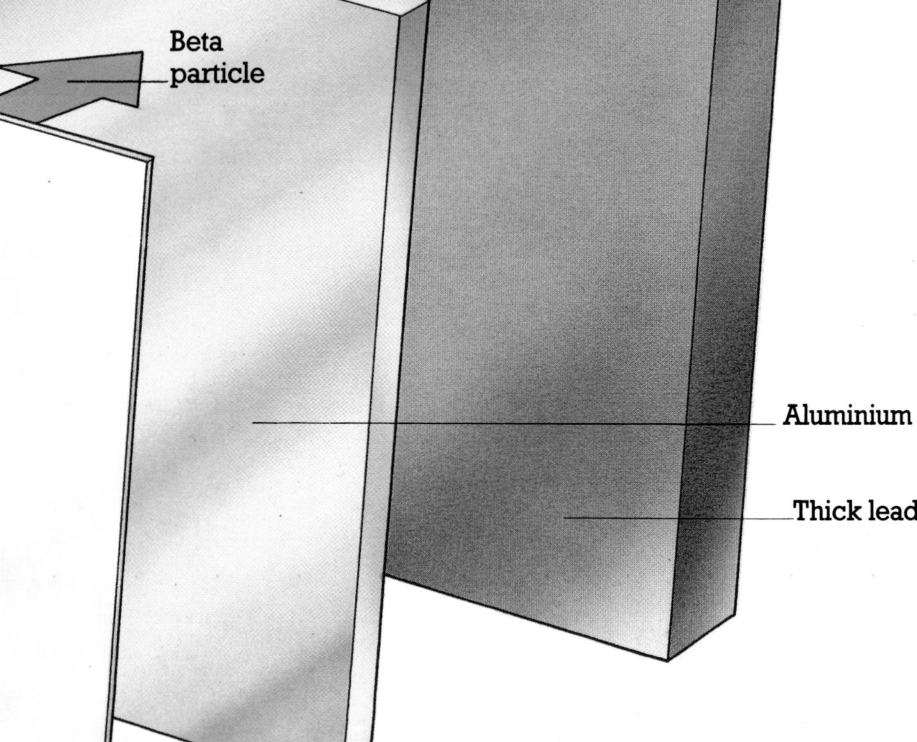

WASTE

The used-up fuel from a nuclear power station is very radioactive. The rods taken from the reactor core contain unused fuel, radioactive products of fission and many other things. Disposing of this waste material is a serious problem. The waste is extremely dangerous and it stays radioactive for a very long time. Some waste products are dangerously radioactive for thousands of years. Used reactor fuel cannot be destroyed. It must be stored where it can do no harm. It is also possible to reprocess some of the fuel. Reprocessing extracts unused uranium from spent fuel. If the fuel has been produced by a fast breeder reactor, reprocessing will also extract plutonium. The uranium and plutonium can then be used again in a reactor.

REPROCESSING

Fuel for reprocessing is transported in special containers known as flasks (right). It can then be held in temporary storage for a time. In the reprocessing plant, useful fuels are extracted by dissolving processes. But there is still a lot of radioactive waste left over that has to be disposed of.

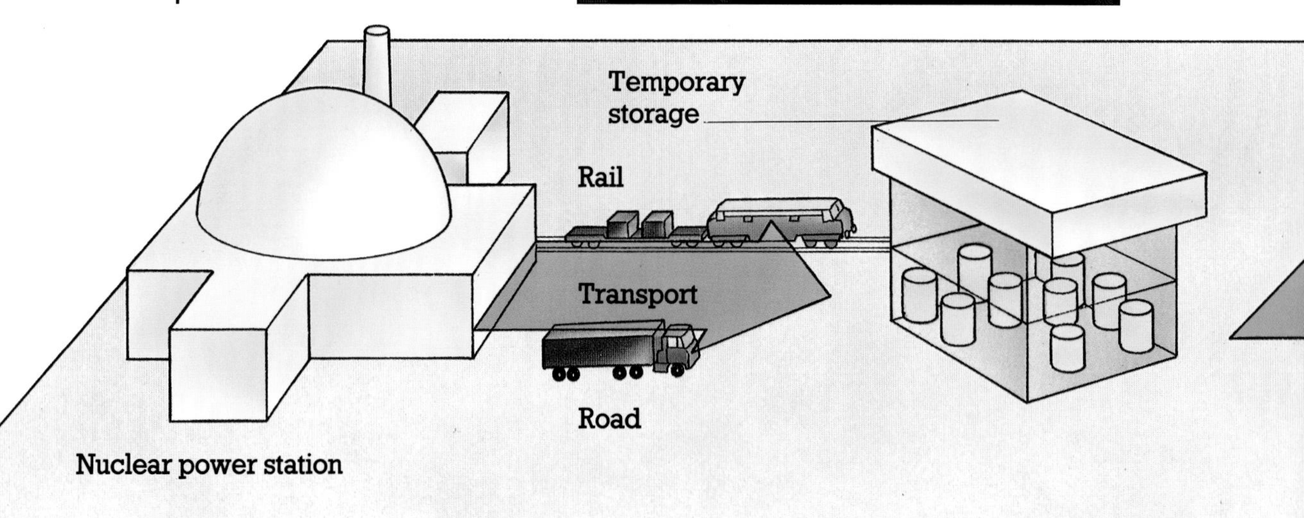

TEMPORARY STORAGE

When used fuel rods are first taken from the reactor, some of the radioactivity dies away quite quickly. Before anything is done with the rods – such as reprocessing – they are stored in water-filled ponds, known as cooling ponds, until they become less radioactive. In some countries, such as the United States, most spent fuel is being kept in such ponds until good ways of disposing of it are found.

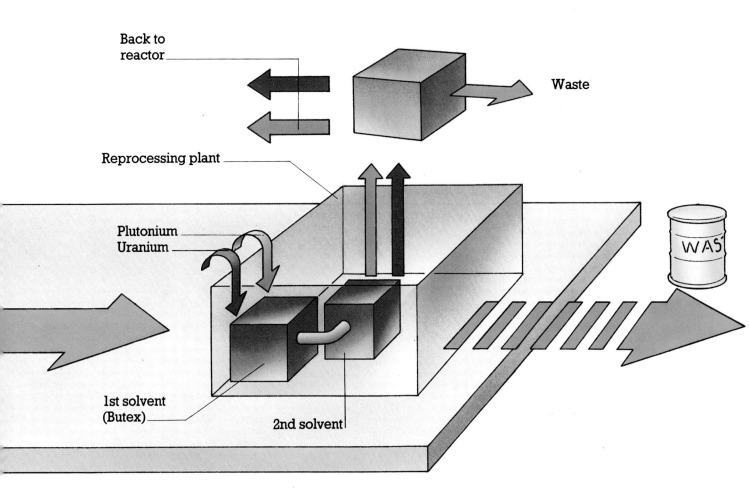

Back to reactor
Waste
Reprocessing plant
Plutonium
Uranium
1st solvent (Butex)
2nd solvent
WAST

WASTE DISPOSAL

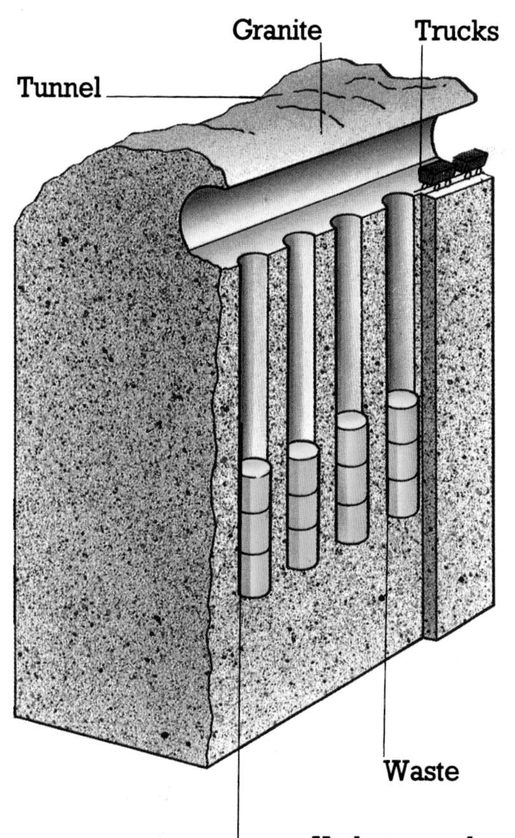

There are three types of waste from nuclear power stations: low-level, intermediate and high-level waste. The level shows how radioactive it is. Things such as cleaning materials and protective clothing that have been exposed to small amounts of radiation in the power station are low-level waste. It is quite easy to dispose of low-level waste by burying it. Intermediate and high-level waste is more of a problem. The most common solution is to put it in sealed containers far underground. This can be done by digging special tunnels, or by putting the waste in disused mines, like the salt mine below.

STORED IN ROCK

The safest way to dispose of intermediate and high-level waste is to put it in sealed containers and bury it. The waste can stay radioactive for thousands of years. Because of this, it is important that the waste is buried in rock that is hard – such as granite – and will not move. If the rock moved or cracked, waste might escape if the waste containers broke. Radioactive material would be released and may be carried into water supplies.

SEA DISPOSAL

Waste is sometimes put in sealed containers and dumped into the sea in places where it is very deep. Usually, only low-level waste is disposed of in this way. Throwing waste into the sea is much cheaper than burying it, but many people are worried about this method. If any containers broke, radioactive material would leak into the sea.

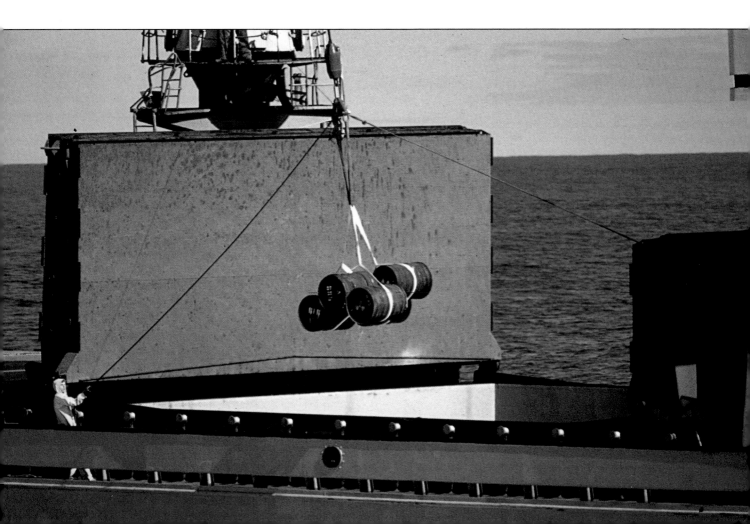

DISASTER

Ever since the explosion of the atom bombs dropped on Hiroshima and Nagasaki in Japan, people have been aware of the terrible destruction and loss of life such bombs can cause. Although there are very strict safety regulations, there is always the possibility of accidents at nuclear power stations. But it is very unlikely that a nuclear reactor will explode like an atom bomb. The most common type of accident is a radiation leak from the power station. If a lot of radiation escapes, it can spread over a wide area. It can be dangerous to people for many years after the accident. Three of the world's worst accidents happened in Britain at Sellafield (1957), in the United States at Three Mile Island (1979) and in the Soviet Union at Chernobyl (1986).

THREE MILE ISLAND

In March 1979, an accident occurred at the United States nuclear plant at Three Mile Island near Harrisburg, Pennsylvania. The reactor core was damaged when the cooling system failed. There was a risk that the whole core would melt and continue reacting. The accident led to doubts in the United States about using nuclear power.

15-kilometre exclusion zone
The milk from cows that have eaten contaminated grass is radioactive and so can affect humans.
When a reactor leaks radiation, pregnant women, babies and young children are particularly at risk.

SELLAFIELD

In 1957, there was a large radiation leak, caused by a fire, at one of Britain's nuclear reactors at Windscale in Cumbria. Radiation spread across England, Wales and northern Europe. Milk from 500 square kilometres around the plant could not be used for a long time. Many facts about the accident were not released until years afterwards. The accident was worse than the one at Three Mile Island, but in 1957 people did not know so much about the dangers. Later, the name of Windscale was changed to Sellafield.

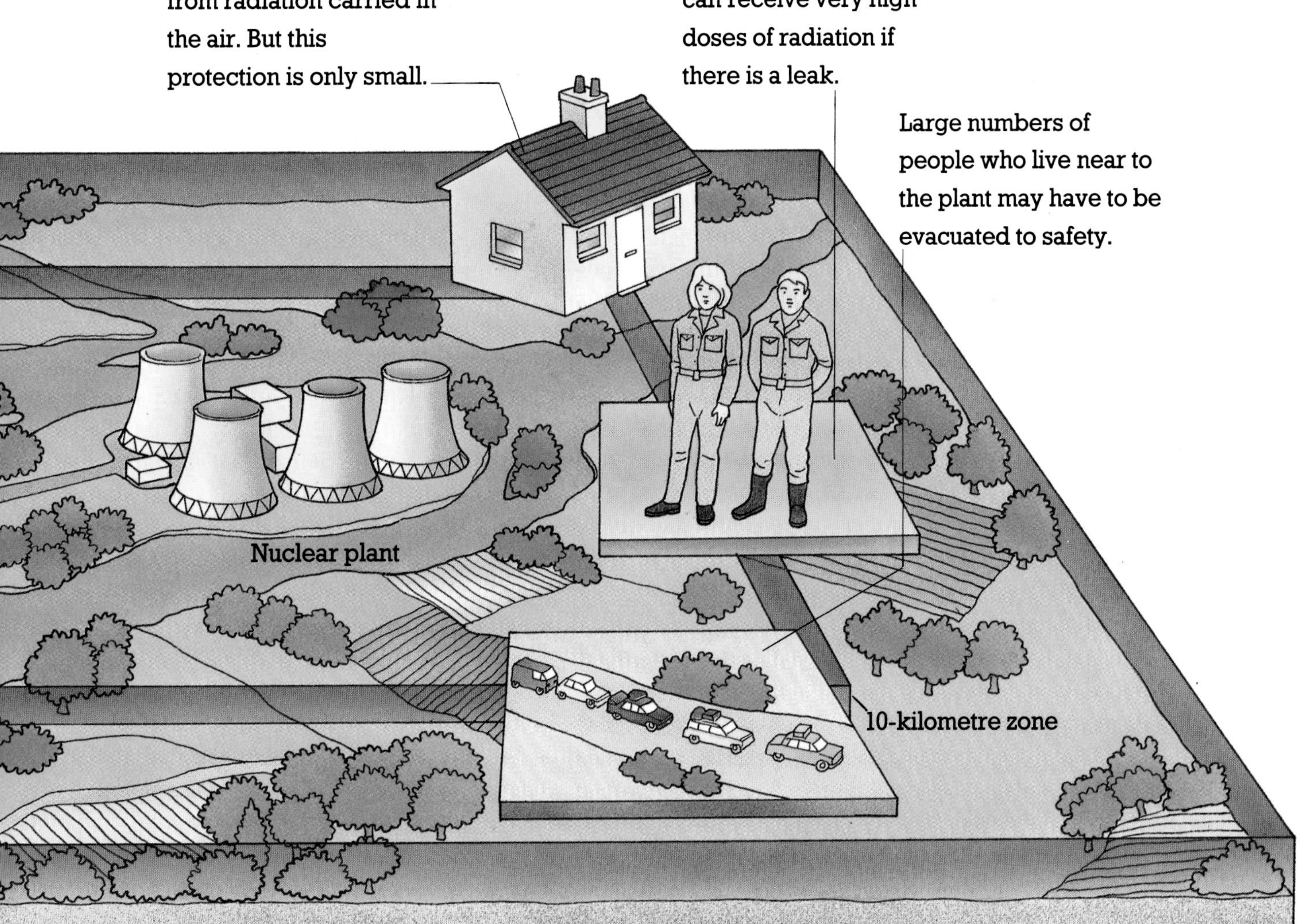

Staying indoors can provide some protection from radiation carried in the air. But this protection is only small.
The people who work at a nuclear power station can receive very high doses of radiation if there is a leak.
Large numbers of people who live near to the plant may have to be evacuated to safety.
Nuclear plant
10-kilometre zone

DISASTER

Break in coolant pipe

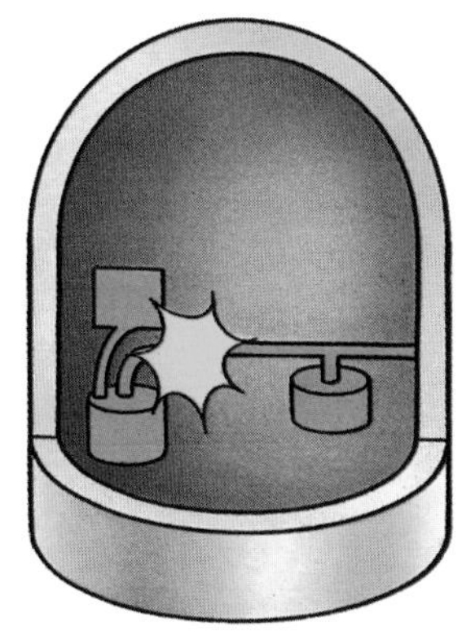

Failure of back up system

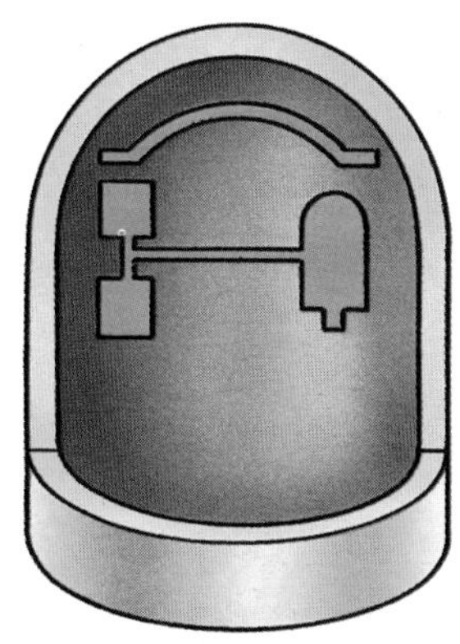

Reactor vessel overheats

Fuel meltdown

HOW THEY HAPPEN

Accidents usually happen when a reactor's cooling system fails. If the back-up cooling system fails as well, the reactor vessel can overheat. If the fuel then starts to melt, the situation becomes very difficult to control.

CHERNOBYL DISASTER

At Chernobyl in the Soviet Union in April 1986, an explosion destroyed the core of the reactor. A very large amount of radiation was released, spreading out over most of Europe, and reaching Sweden within two days.

EFFECTS ON THE BODY

People can become affected by radiation in two ways. They can come into contact with something that is radioactive, or radioactive material carried in the air may get into the body. Radioactive material can stay dangerous for a long time (as is shown in the graph).

Radiation damages the cells of the body. If somebody is exposed to large amounts of radiation, the organs of the body, which are made of cells, can stop working properly. This is known as radiation sickness. Coming into contact with smaller amounts of radiation can cause cancer, which may not appear until many years later.

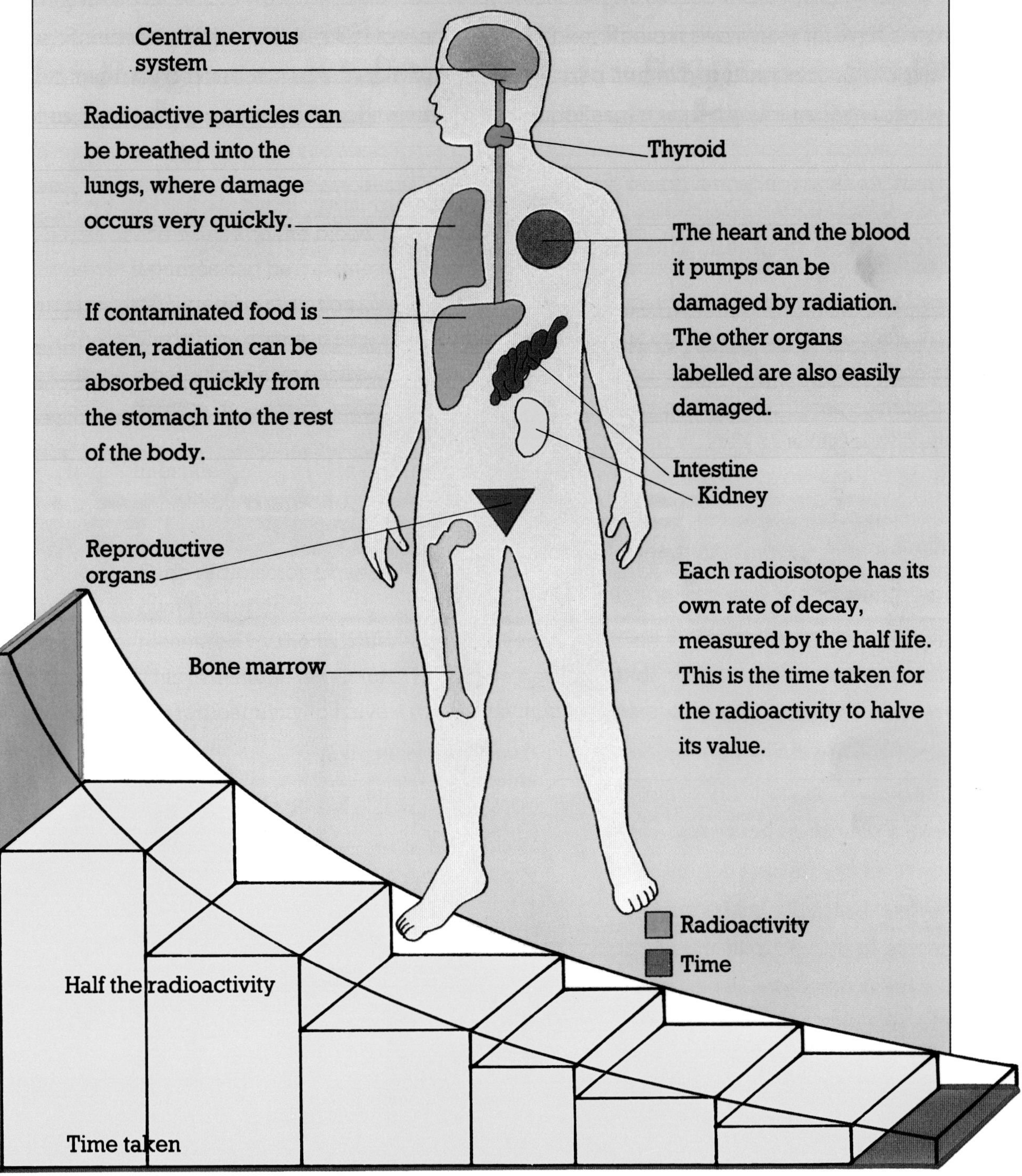

Central nervous system
Radioactive particles can be breathed into the lungs, where damage occurs very quickly.
If contaminated food is eaten, radiation can be absorbed quickly from the stomach into the rest of the body.
Reproductive organs
Bone marrow
Thyroid
The heart and the blood it pumps can be damaged by radiation. The other organs labelled are also easily damaged.
Intestine
Kidney
Each radioisotope has its own rate of decay, measured by the half life. This is the time taken for the radioactivity to halve its value.
Radioactivity
Time
Half the radioactivity
Time taken

ULTIMATE DISASTER

The ultimate disaster with nuclear energy would be a nuclear war. The power in the explosion of nuclear weapons could cause enormous destruction and loss of life. Long after a bomb had exploded, the radiation it had released would be able to cause illness and death. Because of the terrible effects these weapons would have, no country has dared to start a nuclear war. But this does not mean that nobody ever will. A nuclear war could even start by mistake, if somebody gave the wrong command. In a war, most nuclear weapons would be carried to their targets by missiles. But there are also nuclear bombs and even shells to fire from guns. Missiles can be launched from ships, submarines, land vehicles or silos in the ground. Silos protect the missiles from attack.

DELIVERY AND IGNITION

Intercontinental ballistic missiles (ICBMs) can carry several nuclear devices (known as warheads) for thousands of kilometres. ICBMs are divided into "stages". When each stage runs out of fuel it drops off the missile. Finally, when it is over the target area, the missile "bus" releases the warheads. A warhead is detonated by bringing uranium or plutonium very quickly together with a source of neutrons. This starts a very fast uncontrolled nuclear reaction. In the nuclear device in the picture, the neutron source is fired into the plutonium. The plutonium is then crushed onto the neutron by the explosive that surrounds it, causing the nuclear reaction.

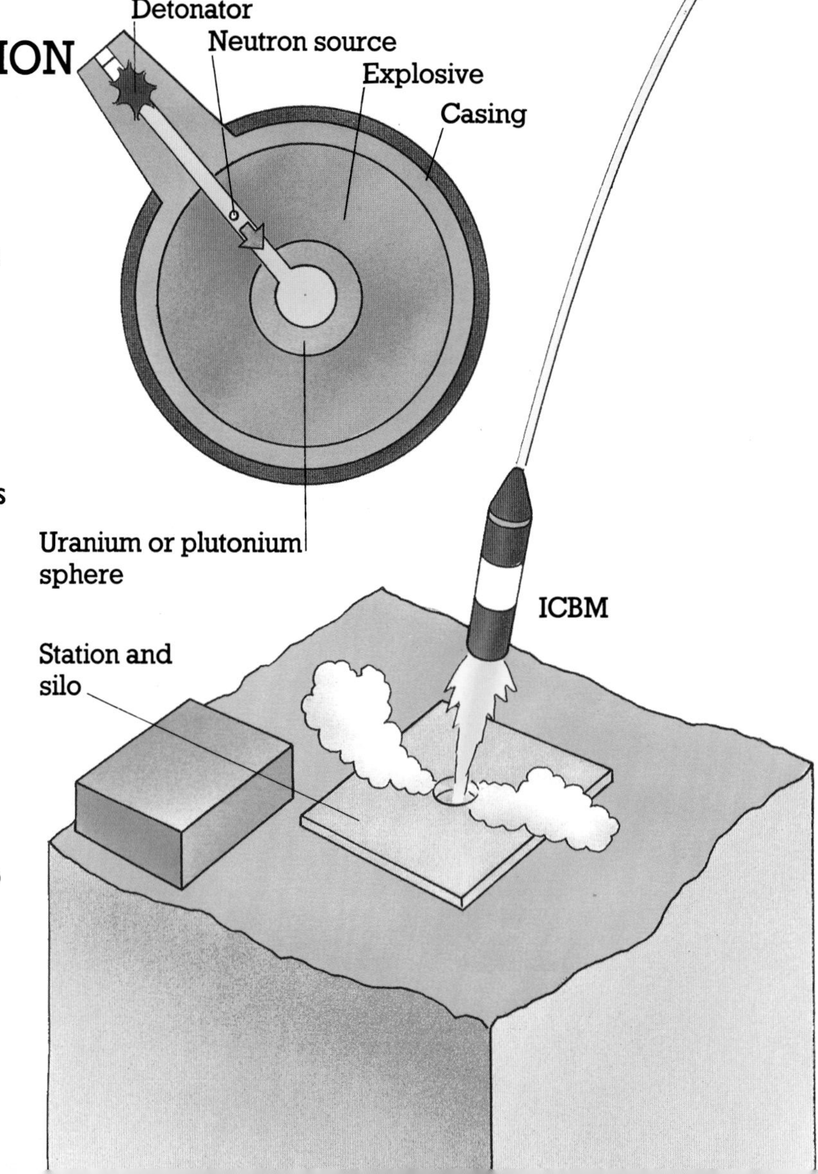

Multiple warheads released

Missile bus

Target zone

First stage

BLAST ZONES

The damage caused by a nuclear explosion can be divided into "blast zones". How big each zone is depends on the power of the weapon. The damage is caused by two things: the blast from the explosion and the heat given off. The radiation given out can also kill or injure many people, as at Hiroshima (left) in 1946.

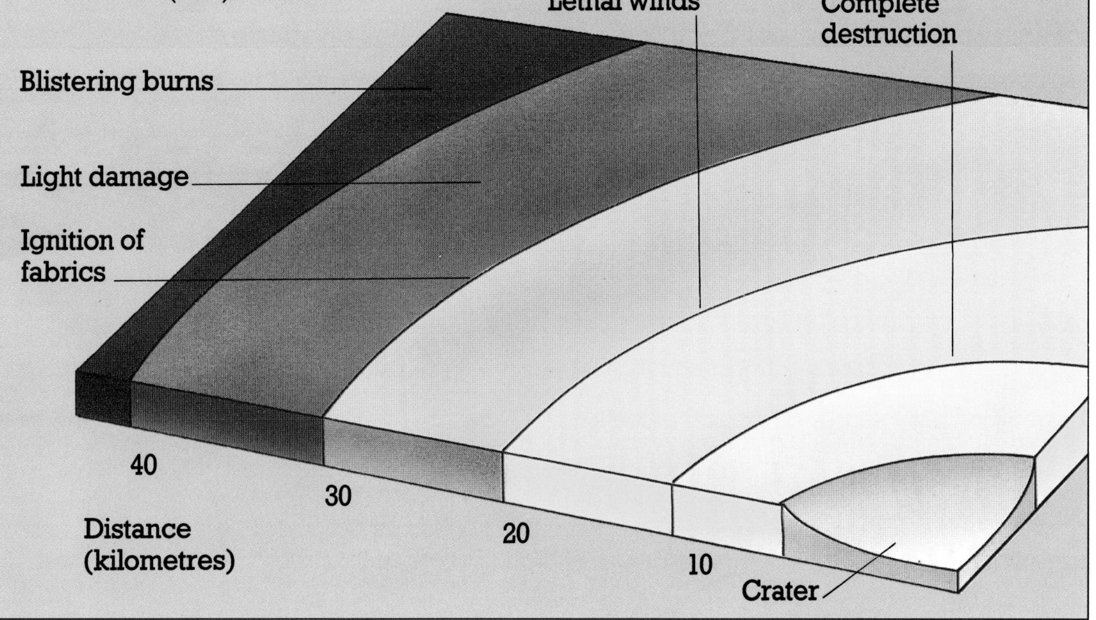

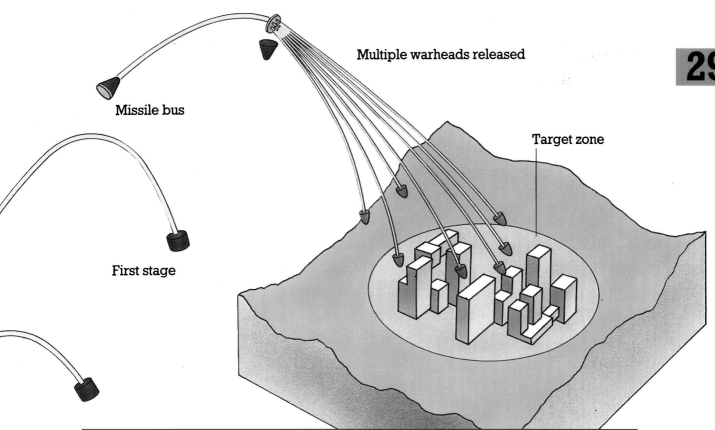

A NUCLEAR FUTURE

Energy supplies are essential for the wealth of any country. Nuclear power seems to provide an almost unlimited source of energy for the future. A number of countries, such as France and the Soviet Union are relying more and more on nuclear energy for their power. And a growing number of less developed countries are starting nuclear programmes. But people have always worried about the dangers of nuclear power. On top of this, it has been found to cost a great deal more to produce than first thought, so many people are now wondering whether any more nuclear power stations should be built. The problems and benefits of using nuclear energy have to be balanced against the alternatives.

ALTERNATIVES

A large part of the world's power comes from fossil fuels (coal, oil and gas) in stations like the one on the right. This causes pollution from the fumes of the burning fuel. Hydroelectric power (water power) causes very little pollution but there are often no suitable supplies of water. Most other sources of power can only provide small amounts.

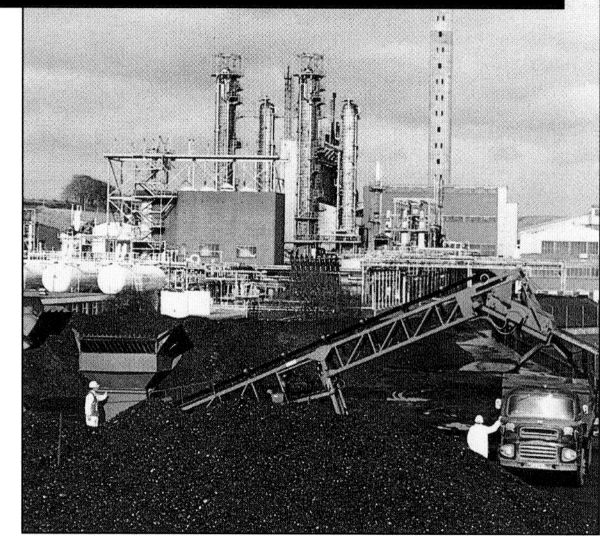

GLOSSARY

breeder reactor nuclear reactor that "breeds" (produces) plutonium. A fast breeder reactor works at very high temperatures and produces plutonium quickly.

conventional power station power station that burns fossil fuels (coal, oil or gas).

fission the splitting of the nucleus of an atom, accompanied by a great release of energy.

isotopes different forms that the nuclei of the atoms of some elements can take. They differ in the number of neutrons they have.

neutron one of the types of subatomic particle that make up the nucleus of an atom. Free-moving neutrons can split certain atoms.

nucleus small, very dense, central part of an atom. Most of the mass of an atom is in the nucleus.

proton A type of subatomic particle. Along with neutrons they make up the nucleus of an atom. The two are held together by an extremely powerful force.

radiation rays or minute particles that carry energy (such as alpha particles or gamma rays). Some radiation occurs naturally.

reactor core part of a nuclear reactor where controlled nuclear fission takes place.

reprocessing extracting useful nuclear fuel, in the form of uranium and plutonium, from fuel that has been used once already.

USEFUL ADDRESSES

Department of Energy,
Thames House South, Millbank,
London, SW1
Telephone: 071-238 3000.

Friends of the Earth,
26-28 Underwood Street,
London N1
Telephone: 071-490 1555

AEA Technology Harwell,
Oxfordshire OX11 0RA
Telephone: 0235 821111
The Atomic Energy Authority

The Nuclear Electricity
Information Group,
22 Buckingham Gate,
London SW1
Telephone: 071-828 8248

INDEX

PRINTED IN BELGIUM BY proost INTERNATIONAL BOOK PRODUCTION